MINDFUL PARENTING TECHNIQUES

A Complete Guide For Nurturing Harmony And Resilience In Your Child's Journey And Cultivating Emotional Intelligence And Mindful Connections

WALTER ZYAIRE

DISCLAIMER

The information in this book is intended only for general informational purposes; it should not be used in lieu of professional advice or medical care. Since the author is not licensed to practice therapy, the information offered should not be used in place of the expertise, judgment, or guidance of qualified mental health or medical professionals. Readers are encouraged to consult therapists, medical specialists, or other qualified authorities regarding their particular situation and needs. The publisher and author disclaim all liability for any actions or decisions taken by readers based on the information in this book. Results may vary from person to person and this book's approaches, procedures, and strategies may not be suitable in all circumstances. Considering unique situations and consulting a qualified expert are essential when choosing the right course of action. Neither the publisher nor the author recommend or guarantee the efficacy of any therapy or treatment that is indicated in this book. Because the information is based on the author's research and understanding at the time of publishing, it could not reflect the most recent developments or practices in the treatment area. The publisher and the author both disclaim all liability for the accuracy, completeness, or use of the material in this book. Readers bear full responsibility for the decisions and actions they choose in light of the information presented in this book.

TABLE OF CONTENTS

 The book "Mindful Parenting Techniques" offers parents a thorough manual for navigating the difficulties of contemporary parenting from a mindfulness perspective. This book is important because it gives parents useful skills and ideas to help them feel better emotionally, communicate better with their kids, and build stronger family bonds. The ideas of mindful parenting grow more and more applicable in today's fast-paced environment, which is full of stressors and diversions. They provide a comprehensive approach to supporting a child's development.

 The book give readers a comprehensive grasp of mindfulness and its tenets while demonstrating how it can be used in parenting. The book makes a strong argument for implementing mindful parenting practices into regular family life by exploring its many advantages. The book walk parents through the process of developing emotional control, mindfulness, and effective communication skills, with a focus on the positive effects these practices can have on family dynamics.

The book's emphasis on incorporating mindfulness into everyday parenting issues is one of its most notable aspects. The book provides useful suggestions that are in line with the realities of parenting, from handling sleep problems and scholastic stress to handling tantrums and emotional outbursts. In addition, research into developing emotional intelligence in kids and cultivating mindful interactions within the family shows a dedication to supporting holistic development.

The addition on mindful parenting in the digital age recognizes the particular difficulties brought about by technology and offers suggestions for fostering positive interactions between kids and screens. Furthermore, the book emphasizes the significance of self-care for parents, acknowledging the necessity of striking a balance between personal well-being and parenting obligations.

"Mindful Parenting Techniques" is a noteworthy tool for parents looking to raise their kids with consideration and purpose. Through the perspective of mindfulness, the book addresses several facets of parenting and provides parents with the necessary tools to create a resilient and caring family atmosphere in the fast-paced world of today.

CHAPTER ONE

OVERVIEW OF MINDFUL PARENTING TECHNIQUES

COMPREHENDING MINDFUL PARENTING

In the complex fabric of parenting, mindful parenting is a notion that has been increasingly popular recently. This parenting style, which has its roots in mindfulness, emphasizes developing a sharper awareness of the present moment to build a stronger bond with the kid and with the parent. In contrast to traditional parenting approaches, which frequently emphasize routines and restrictions, mindful parenting encourages parents to interact with their kids more intentionally and thoughtfully.

The process of applying mindfulness concepts to the difficulties and rewards of childrearing is known as mindful parenting. It is influenced by mindfulness techniques, which have long been a part of contemplative traditions like Buddhism.

Being present, embracing oneself and one's thoughts and feelings without passing judgment, and adopting a welcoming and non-reactive attitude toward situations are the cornerstones of mindfulness. When it comes to parenting, this idea supports more sensitive and caring interactions between parents and their kids.

THE VALUE OF MINDFUL PARENTING IN THE MODERN AGE

In the technologically advanced and fast-paced world of today, the value of mindful parenting is becoming more and more clear. It can be difficult to manage the intricacies of family dynamics when parents and children are disconnected due to the pressures and diversions of contemporary living. These problems can be solved by mindful parenting, which encourages purposeful and meaningful relationships. It motivates parents to schedule meaningful time with their children, resulting in a better comprehension of their individual needs, feelings, and viewpoints.

The development of emotional intelligence in both parents and children is one of the most important components of mindful parenting. Parents can provide a good example for their children in healthy emotional control by becoming conscious of their feelings. Children can then use this to learn how to manage their own emotions healthily.

As the importance of emotional intelligence in determining success and well-being grows, mindful parenting becomes a useful strategy for giving kids the life skills they need.

In addition, the mindful parenting technique's focus on non-judgmental awareness inspires parents to approach their parenting journey with self-compassion. Being a parent is a complicated and frequently difficult task, but mindful parenting offers parents a framework to handle the ups and downs that are unavoidable with grace and acceptance. This strategy can help create a more loving and healthy family environment and lessen the stress that parents face.

Practicing mindful parenting is adopting a kind and all-encompassing parenting style. As we examine the significance of mindful parenting in the contemporary era, it is clear that this paradigm shift provides a way to develop resilient, emotionally intelligent people who are better able to deal with the challenges of the modern world in addition to providing a way to strengthen the parent-child bond.

CHAPTER TWO

THE BASIS OF CONSCIENTIOUS PARENTING

THE MEANING AND FOUNDATIONS OF MINDFULNESS

The practice of mindfulness has its origins in old contemplative traditions, especially Buddhism, and has been incorporated into contemporary parenting and psychology. Fundamentally, mindfulness is practicing acute awareness and present in the here and now, judgment-free. It is a fundamental instrument for developing a closer relationship with oneself and one's children in the context of parenting.

The development of intention, attitude, and attention are central to the mindfulness tenets. Focus is purposefully placed on the interactions and experiences that are taking place right now. This entails recognizing ideas and feelings without passing judgment and practicing nonjudgmental awareness.

By embracing compassion and acceptance, the mindfulness mindset creates an atmosphere that supports the emotional and psychological well-being of both parents and children.

TECHNIQUES FOR HANDLING THE STRESS OF PARENTING

An unavoidable part of being a parent is experiencing stress. For parents and kids to live in a supportive and healthy environment, effective stress management is essential. One might use a variety of coping mechanisms to manage parental stress. One such tactic is to use mindfulness activities, like deep breathing exercises or meditation, to create a sense of centering and calmness in the middle of chaos.

Building a robust support system is also essential. Talking to friends, relatives, or support groups about their struggles and experiences can be beneficial for parents. Stress can be reduced by asking for help when you need it, whether it be in the form of child care or emotional support. Parents who are good at managing their time can prioritize and arrange their tasks to prevent feeling overburdened. In the end, stress reduction is greatly aided by taking a holistic approach to self-care, which includes getting enough sleep, exercising frequently, and leading a balanced lifestyle.

BUILDING PARENTAL EMOTIONAL RESILIENCE

Effective parenting is based on emotional resilience, which gives parents the tools they need to deal with obstacles and failures with grace and flexibility. Promoting emotional resilience in parents entails developing a positive outlook and coping skills that help them overcome challenging circumstances. Emotional resilience is largely dependent on the development of a strong parent-child link since a stable attachment offers both parties a sense of security and support.

Fostering candid dialogue among family members creates a secure environment for sharing feelings and working together to solve problems. By enabling kids to actively manage their emotions, emotional regulation education promotes a positive family dynamic. Adopting a growth mindset, which regards obstacles as chances for education and development, helps parents and kids alike become resilient.

Parents' road toward emotional regulation entails identifying and comprehending their feelings, using practical stress-reduction techniques, and actively fostering emotional resilience throughout the parenting journey. For both parents and children, this all-encompassing strategy helps to create a nurturing and emotionally supporting atmosphere.

CHAPTER THREE

COMMUNICATING MINDFULLY WITH YOUR CHILD

SKILLS OF ACTIVE LISTENING

Having thoughtful conversations with your child is essential to building a strong and happy bond between you two. The ability to actively listen is essential to this process. When you listen to your child actively, you give their words your whole attention and do not pass judgment or make interruptions.

Giving your child your whole attention, keeping eye contact, and nodding to indicate comprehension allows them to freely express themselves.

This shows your child that their opinions and feelings are respected and aids in the development of trust.

DEMONSTRATING COMPASSION AND PERCEPTION

An additional essential component of mindful communication with your child is expressing understanding and empathy. Empathy is recognizing your child's feelings, respecting their experiences, and placing yourself in their position. By demonstrating empathy, you establish a bond that promotes emotional stability. Even if you disagree with your child's point of view, it is important to let them know that their sentiments are understood and valued. This promotes candid communication and makes it easier for your kid to open up to you about their feelings.

PARENTING THROUGH NONVIOLENT COMMUNICATION

Parenting with nonviolent communication is a powerful concept that highlights the value of expressing oneself without using blame or hostility. Marshall Rosenberg's approach enables parents to express their wants, feelings, and worries in a straightforward and nonjudgmental way. Nonviolent communication fosters a courteous and encouraging environment by concentrating on the consequences of behavior rather than making judgments. By teaching kids to express themselves similarly, this method promotes a cooperative and understanding home environment.

Using "I" words to communicate your wants and feelings instead of blaming your child is a key component of nonviolent communication practice. Saying something like, "I need a tidy space to relax, and I feel frustrated when the toys are not put away because it creates clutter in the living room," expresses your needs and sentiments without criticizing your child.

This method fosters a cooperative problem-solving mindset in which parents and children cooperate to identify solutions that satisfy everyone's requirements.

Practicing peaceful communication techniques, demonstrating empathy and compassion, and improving active listening abilities are all essential components of mindful communication with your child. By implementing these ideas into your parenting style, you build a solid, trustworthy bond with your child and encourage a communicative and supportive family environment.

CHAPTER FOUR

BUILDING INTENTIONAL BONDS WITHIN THE FAMILY

DEVELOPING A RELATIONSHIP WITH YOUR CHILD

Building a strong and meaningful bond with your child is essential to creating a thoughtful relationship. The first step in building this relationship is to just be there for your child, giving them your whole attention. Setting out time for one-on-one conversations is crucial in the hectic world we live in. Strong parent-child relationships are built on being aware of your child's needs and feelings, whether through shared activities, chats, or even quiet times.

Establishing this relationship is largely dependent on effective communication. It's important to validate your child's experiences and feelings by actively listening to them. Establishing an environment that is judgment-free and open to communication allows your child to freely express their ideas, worries, and joys. Developing an atmosphere of trust and understanding through mindful communication also entails being conscious of your reactions and feelings.

MINDFULLY DEVELOPING SIBLING RELATIONSHIPS

Fostering mindfulness within these dynamics is essential to promoting harmony and mutual understanding in sibling relationships, which can be both rewarding and demanding. It is fundamental to foster empathy and respect among siblings. By helping their kids to recognize and value each other's individuality, parents can promote a spirit of friendship rather than rivalry.

Teaching children how to resolve conflicts and guiding siblings through arguments in a positive way are also aspects of mindful parenting. Fostering a cooperative family environment that prioritizes collaboration over rivalry strengthens the link between siblings.

Modeling and promoting deeds of compassion and support is crucial for fostering the belief that siblings are allies in the process of growing up.

REBUILDING THE PARENT-CHILD RELATIONSHIP

It takes deliberate effort and mindfulness to strengthen the parent-child relationship, which is a continuous process. It takes a consistent emotional presence to make youngsters feel safe and cherished. This calls for both physical presence and emotional awareness of your child's needs. Taking sensitive cues from them and acting on them helps establish a solid foundation of trust.

Another component of mindful parenting is establishing clear and reasonable expectations. This entails appreciating your child's uniqueness, appreciating their strengths, and offering advice without placing unreasonably high expectations. No matter how big or small, your child's accomplishments will be recognized and celebrated, which will boost their self-esteem and the parent-child bond.

The relationship between parents and children can also be strengthened by establishing customs and rituals inside the household. Whether it's a weekly game night, dinners together, or special trips, these occasions generate enduring memories and strengthen the bond of family.

CHAPTER FIVE

CONSCIOUS GUIDANCE AND DISCIPLINE

TRANSITIONING FROM PENALTIES TO REPRIMANDS

A fundamental change in how difficult conduct is addressed is required for mindful discipline; punishing methods must give way to more helpful and compassionate forms of instruction. Rather than employing punishment as a tool for control, mindful discipline emphasizes comprehending the underlying reasons behind conduct and aims to equip kids with the knowledge and skills necessary to make wise decisions. This change is based on the idea that discipline tries to support a child's emotional and cognitive growth, while punishment frequently falls short of addressing the underlying causes of misbehavior.

Children can learn and develop in a more supportive and favorable environment when caregivers and educators reframe discipline as a teaching tool rather than a punitive one. This method encourages adults to support children with empathy and compassion as they navigate difficult emotions and situations, acknowledging that children may not always have the appropriate abilities. Creating an environment where mistakes are viewed as chances for growth rather than as grounds for punishment, encouraging open communication, and placing an emphasis on learning opportunities are all part of the process of moving from punishment to discipline.

INSTILLING A COMPASSIONATE TEACHING OF RESPONSIBILITY

Teaching responsibility and developing compassion go hand in hand in the context of mindful discipline. By encouraging a feeling of accountability in children, caregivers and educators can empower them to take ownership of their activities instead of enforcing rules and expecting compliance. This entails educating kids about the effects of their decisions on both themselves and other people. Adults may help children think critically about their actions, recognize the potential effects on others, and take action to make apologies by providing them with compassionate counsel.

It is also acknowledged that children's capacity for emotional control and decision-making is still developing when they are taught responsibility with compassion. It entails giving them the resources and assistance they require to overcome obstacles. Caregivers and educators may foster an atmosphere where children feel comfortable admitting their mistakes, learning from them, and striving to make better decisions in the future by prioritizing understanding over punishment. This method builds a foundation for responsible behavior by encouraging self-discipline and autonomy.

CREATING MINDFUL BOUNDARIES

Setting boundaries with awareness entails taking a deliberate and careful approach to creating rules that provide a secure and caring environment for kids.

Conscious discipline encourages adults to jointly set limits with children, taking into account their unique needs and developmental stages, as opposed to enforcing strict rules through punishment. While acknowledging the necessity of boundaries in establishing a feeling of security, this method also emphasizes the value of flexibility and understanding in how they are applied.

Setting boundaries with awareness requires open communication to make sure kids know why certain rules exist. Additionally, it encourages children to take part in decision-making when it is appropriate, which helps them develop a feeling of accountability and ownership. Caretakers and educators can provide a framework that directs behavior while providing opportunities for inquiry and development by carefully defining boundaries. This method emphasizes the value of flexibility in discipline by acknowledging that boundaries are dynamic and may need to be adjusted as children grow and learn.

CHAPTER SIX

INCLUDING MINDFULNESS IN EVERYDAY PARENTING DIFFICULTIES

HANDLING TEMPER TANTRUMS AND EMOTIONAL EXPLOSIONS

Developing awareness and a nonjudgmental presence is a key component of incorporating mindfulness into parenting, particularly during trying times like tantrums and emotional outbursts. A mindful approach urges parents to wait before acting impulsively in response to their child's strong emotions. Parents who pause to notice their feelings and thoughts are better able to respond with empathy and understanding.

By teaching parents to accept their child's emotions without passing judgment, mindfulness fosters a secure environment where emotions can be expressed. Parents who want to stay present during a tantrum can practice deep breathing or grounding techniques instead of trying to stop it right away.

This thoughtful reaction not only aids in defusing the situation but also encourages emotional control in both the parent and the youngster.

HANDLING SLEEP PROBLEMS CONSCIOUSLY

Understanding the significance of a calm and leisurely bedtime routine is a prerequisite for integrating mindfulness into the treatment of sleep problems. Reduce distractions and create a calming bedtime routine as part of mindful parenting to promote a sleep-friendly atmosphere. This may include activities like reading a relaxing story, practicing gentle stretches, or engaging in deep-breathing exercises together.

Mindful awareness extends to acknowledging the child's distinct sleep habits and demands. Instead of rigorously imposing a particular bedtime, parents can watch their child's natural sleep routine and modify it accordingly.

Mindfulness also plays a role in regulating the unavoidable interruptions that may occur during the night, developing a patient and understanding reaction to midnight awakenings.

HANDLING HOMEWORK AND ACADEMIC STRESS

Mindful parenting understands the possible pressures associated with academics and homework, emphasizing the need to foster a supportive and nurturing learning environment. When assisting with homework, parents can bring mindfulness into the equation by encouraging a focused and present mindset.

This involves minimizing distractions, being fully engaged in the task at hand, and fostering a positive attitude towards the learning process.

In moments of academic stress, mindful parenting encourages open communication and active listening. By creating a non-judgmental space for their child to express concerns and frustrations, parents can better understand and address the root causes of stress.

Mindfulness techniques, such as mindful breathing or short breaks during study sessions, can also be integrated to alleviate tension and promote a balanced approach to academic challenges.

Integrating mindfulness into daily parenting challenges involves a commitment to staying present, fostering understanding, and responding with compassion. By incorporating mindful practices, parents can navigate tantrums, sleep issues, and academic stress in a way that promotes emotional well-being and strengthens the parent-child connection.

CHAPTER SEVEN

NURTURING YOUR CHILD'S EMOTIONAL INTELLIGENCE

DEVELOPING EMOTIONAL AWARENESS IN CHILDREN

Developing Emotional Awareness in children is a crucial aspect of nurturing their emotional intelligence. It involves helping them recognize and understand their own emotions as well as those of others. Parents and caregivers play a pivotal role in creating a supportive environment where children feel safe expressing their feelings. Through open communication, children can learn to identify various emotions, such as joy, anger, sadness, and fear, and understand that these feelings are a natural part of the human experience. By acknowledging and validating their emotions, parents can foster emotional awareness and teach children how to navigate and manage their feelings effectively.

TEACHING MINDFULNESS TO CHILDREN

Teaching Mindfulness to children is another powerful tool in promoting emotional intelligence. Mindfulness involves being present in the moment without judgment, allowing individuals to observe their thoughts and emotions without becoming overwhelmed by them. Introducing mindfulness practices to children can enhance their ability to stay calm in challenging situations, improve focus, and regulate their emotions.

Simple mindfulness exercises, such as deep breathing or guided visualization, can be incorporated into daily routines or bedtime rituals. By instilling mindfulness early on, parents help children develop lifelong skills for emotional regulation and self-awareness.

ENCOURAGING EMPATHY AND COMPASSION

Encouraging empathy and compassion is an integral part of fostering emotional intelligence in children.

Empathy involves understanding and sharing the feelings of others, while compassion goes a step further by motivating individuals to take action to alleviate someone else's suffering.

Parents can nurture empathy in their children by modeling empathetic behavior, actively listening to their concerns, and discussing the feelings of characters in stories or real-life situations. Engaging in acts of kindness and emphasizing the importance of helping others cultivates a sense of compassion in children. These qualities not only contribute to the child's emotional well-being but also lay the foundation for positive social interactions and relationships.

Nurturing a child's emotional intelligence involves a multifaceted approach that encompasses developing emotional awareness, teaching mindfulness, and encouraging empathy and compassion. By creating a supportive and open environment, parents and caregivers can empower children to understand, manage, and connect with their emotions healthily and constructively. These skills not only contribute to the child's personal growth but also play a vital role in shaping their ability to navigate the complexities of interpersonal relationships and thrive in various aspects of life.

CHAPTER EIGHT

MINDFUL PARENTING IN THE DIGITAL AGE

BALANCING SCREEN TIME AND OUTDOOR ACTIVITIES

In the digital age, mindful parenting has become increasingly essential, requiring parents to navigate the delicate balance between allowing their children to engage with technology and ensuring they develop a holistic lifestyle. One crucial aspect of this balance is managing screen time and encouraging outdoor activities. Striking a harmonious equilibrium between the two is essential for the overall well-being of children. While screens offer valuable educational resources and entertainment, excessive screen time can hinder physical activity and social interaction. Mindful parents must actively promote a balance, fostering both the benefits of technology and the joys of outdoor exploration.

TEACHING DIGITAL ETIQUETTE MINDFULLY

Teaching digital etiquette is another pivotal aspect of mindful parenting in the digital age. As children become immersed in the online world, it becomes imperative to instill a sense of responsibility and respect for others in their digital interactions.

Mindful parents engage in open conversations about the impact of words and actions online, emphasizing the importance of kindness and empathy. By nurturing digital etiquette, parents contribute to the development of responsible digital citizens, ensuring their children navigate the virtual realm with integrity and thoughtfulness.

DEVELOPING A POSITIVE CONNECTION WITH TECHNOLOGY

is a continuous process that demands mindful awareness from parents. It involves modeling positive behavior by setting boundaries on their own screen time, which serves as a powerful example for children. Mindful parents consciously integrate technology into family life, using it as a tool for connection rather than a barrier. This approach involves fostering open communication about the role of technology, its limitations, and the impact it can have on relationships. By embracing technology mindfully, parents can guide their children in developing a balanced and respectful relationship with the digital world.

Moreover, the concept of mindful parenting extends beyond merely monitoring and regulating screen time. It involves actively participating in children's digital experiences, and showing genuine interest in their online activities. By engaging in joint digital exploration, parents can better understand the content that captivates their children and identify potential concerns. This collaborative approach facilitates trust and open communication, allowing parents to guide their children in making informed choices about their digital engagements.

Mindful parenting in the digital age encompasses a holistic approach that addresses various aspects of a child's relationship with technology. Balancing screen time with outdoor activities, teaching digital etiquette, and fostering a healthy relationship with technology are interwoven components of a comprehensive strategy. Mindful parents, by staying attuned to their children's digital experiences, can nurture responsible and balanced individuals who navigate the digital landscape with consciousness and integrity.

CHAPTER NINE

MINDFUL SELF-CARE FOR PARENTS

PRIORITIZING SELF-CARE IN PARENTING

Prioritizing self-care in parenting is a crucial concept that acknowledges the significance of maintaining one's well-being amidst the demands of raising children. It involves recognizing the importance of self-nurturing activities and intentionally incorporating them into daily routines. Parents often find themselves immersed in the responsibilities of caring for their children, which can lead to neglecting their own needs. By prioritizing self-care, parents can cultivate a healthier mindset, emotional resilience, and increased energy to meet the challenges of parenting.

FINDING BALANCE BETWEEN PARENTING AND PERSONAL LIFE

Finding a balance between parenting and personal life is a delicate equilibrium that parents strive to achieve.

It requires a mindful approach to time management and the recognition that personal pursuits and interests contribute positively to overall well-being. Balancing responsibilities as a parent with individual needs involves setting boundaries, both with work and family obligations.

This balance is dynamic and may evolve as children grow and family dynamics change. Parents need to communicate openly with their partners and support each other in maintaining a harmonious equilibrium between family life and personal fulfillment.

BUILDING A SUPPORTIVE COMMUNITY

Building a supportive community is a cornerstone of mindful self-care for parents. The proverbial "it takes a village to raise a child" underscores the significance of a strong support system. This community may include family members, friends, neighbors, or fellow parents who share similar experiences. Engaging with a supportive community provides parents with opportunities for mutual assistance, shared resources, and the exchange of valuable advice. Connecting with others who understand the challenges of parenthood fosters a sense of belonging and reduces feelings of isolation, promoting emotional well-being.

Establishing a support network also involves reaching out for help when needed. Whether it's asking a friend to babysit for a few hours or seeking guidance from a parenting group, recognizing the value of communal support is integral to maintaining a healthy balance.

By building connections with others who empathize with the joys and struggles of parenthood, parents can navigate challenges more effectively and create a nurturing environment for both themselves and their children.

In conclusion, the concepts of prioritizing self-care in parenting, finding balance between parenting and personal life, and building a supportive community are interconnected elements that contribute to the overall well-being of parents.

By embracing these principles, parents can cultivate resilience, foster positive relationships, and create a sustainable foundation for both their personal growth and the nurturing of their children.